THE MIRACLE
ON ICE

by Brian Trusdell

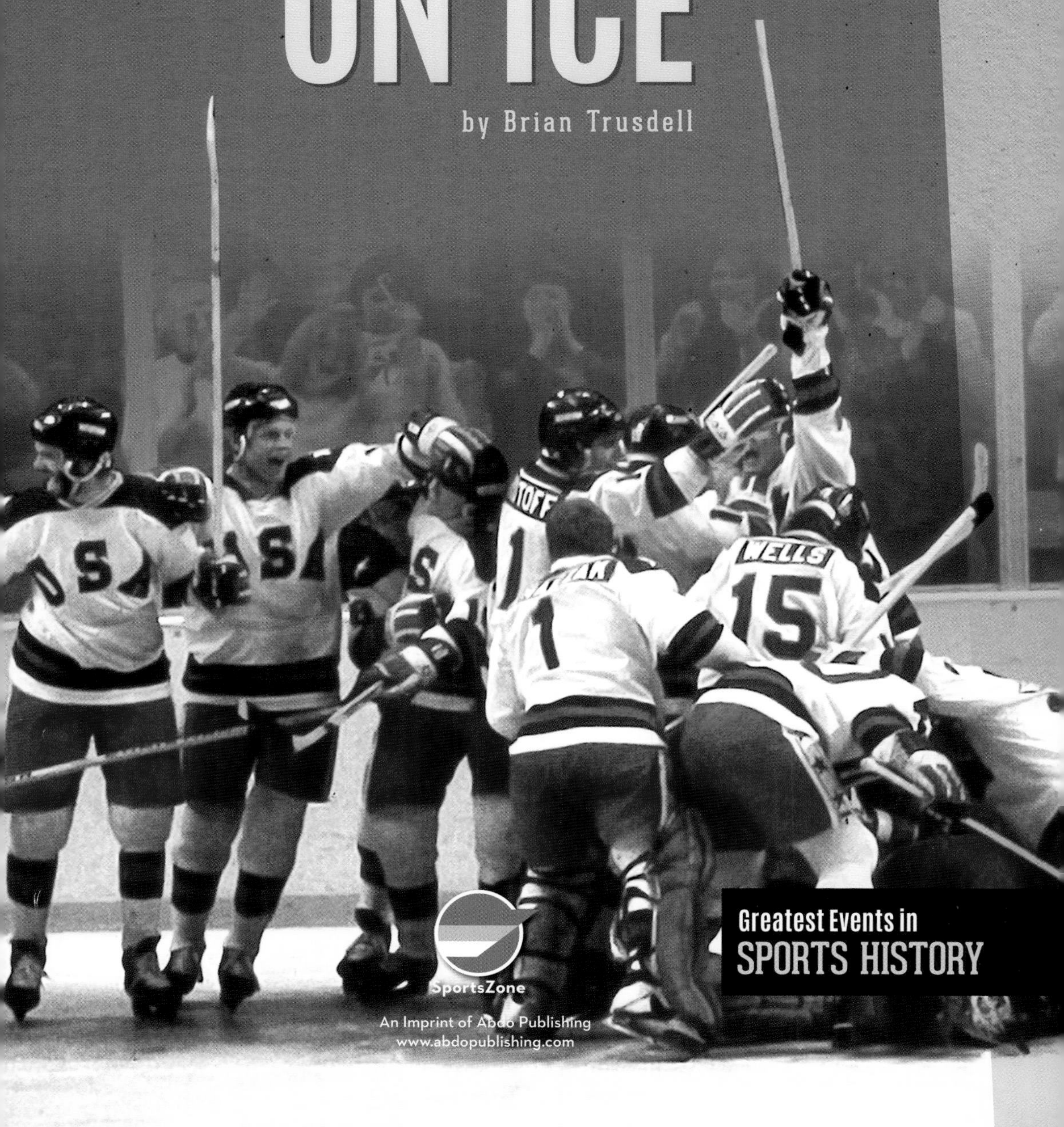

SportsZone
An Imprint of Abdo Publishing
www.abdopublishing.com

SportsZone
An Imprint of Abdo Publishing
www.abdopublishing.com

Greatest Events in
SPORTS HISTORY

www.abdopublishing.com

Published by Abdo Publishing, a division of ABDO, PO Box 398166, Minneapolis, Minnesota 55439. Copyright © 2015 by Abdo Consulting Group, Inc. International copyrights reserved in all countries. No part of this book may be reproduced in any form without written permission from the publisher. SportsZone™ is a trademark and logo of Abdo Publishing.

Printed in the United States of America, North Mankato, Minnesota
102014
012015

Cover Photo: AP Images
Interior Photos: AP Images, 1, 16, 22, 24, 26, 29, 32, 37; Dale G. Young/AP Images, 4; Ron Frehm/AP Images, 7; Douglas Ball/AP Images, 9; Wally McNamee/Corbis, 10; Bill Kostroun/AP Images, 15; B Bennett/Getty Images, 21; Galen Rowell/Corbis, 30, 34; Jerry Cooke/Corbis, 38; Guichard-Rancinan/Sygma/Corbis, 41; Laura Rauch/AP Images, 43

Editor: Chrös McDougall
Series Designer: Craig Hinton

Library of Congress Control Number: 2014944197

Cataloging-in-Publication Data
Trusdell, Brian.
 The miracle on ice / Brian Trusdell.
  p. cm. -- (Greatest events in sports history)
ISBN 978-1-62403-597-5 (lib. bdg.)
Includes bibliographical references and index.
1. Hockey--United States--History--Juvenile literature. 2. Hockey teams--United States--Juvenile literature. 3. Olympic Winter Games (13th : 1980 : Lake Placid, N.Y.)--Juvenile literature. I. Title.
796.962--dc23

2014944197

CONTENTS

US President Jimmy Carter delivers his famous speech on July 15, 1979.

A Troubled Time

Olympic hockey was not on many people's minds on July 15, 1979. It was a Sunday night. People throughout the United States were uncertain about the future. Many people didn't have jobs. Prices of everyday products were going up. Meanwhile, tensions were high between the world's two superpowers, the United States and the Soviet Union. Their indirect "Cold War" had been threatening to turn into a real war since the end of World War II (1939–1945). Then some Middle Eastern countries had refused to sell oil to the United States. That caused an oil shortage throughout the country. Oil is needed to make gas. Cars lined up for hours to refuel. So on that Sunday night, many people tuned in to watch President Carter give a televised speech. The country faced a "crisis of confidence," he said.

ENERGY CRISIS

President Carter's 1979 speech followed an energy crisis. A lot of the world's oil comes from the Middle East. In 1979, a revolution in Iran forced that country's leader to flee. The country became unstable. It slowed the amount of oil it sent around the world drastically. This led to increased gas prices in the United States and elsewhere. Another earlier energy crisis had occurred in 1973. Israel battled its neighboring Arab countries in the Yom Kippur War. The United States supplied Israel with weapons and equipment for the war. Many Middle Eastern countries were upset about this. So they refused to sell oil to the United States or its allies.

"The erosion of our confidence in the future is threatening to destroy the social and the political fabric of America," he said.

Herb Brooks had his own problems that summer. The University of Minnesota men's hockey coach had been hired to coach the US Olympic team. The 1980 Olympic Winter Games would be held in Lake Placid, New York. Brooks had less than a year to build his squad.

Few liked his chances of leading Team USA to a medal. The Soviet Union was dominant in international hockey. It had won each of the previous four Olympic gold medals. Czechoslovakia had won a medal in each of those Winter Games. Meanwhile, Team USA won only a single medal, a silver, during that time. The Soviets and Czechs also had an advantage in selecting players. Rules at the time limited Olympic competition to amateurs. In the United States,

Herb Brooks coached the University of Minnesota hockey team before taking over the 1980 US Olympic team.

the best athletes were professionals. They were paid to compete in the National Hockey League (NHL). So Brooks was limited mostly to college players. But the Soviets, Czechs, and other communist countries had their choice of players. That's because those countries provided jobs for the best athletes. Those athletes barely worked at all. Instead they spent most of their time training for sports. But technically the athletes were paid for the jobs, not their sports. That allowed the athletes to keep their amateur status.

IN THE News

President Jimmy Carter gave his famous televised speech on July 15, 1979. *TIME* magazine wrote about the mood of the country around that time.

> *For some time past, but more sharply this summer, the US has been slipping into a morass of interrelated problems. One is the energy crisis, marked by its gas lines and soaring prices. One is the painful combination of inflation and economic stagnation. One is the widespread perception that Jimmy Carter has seemed unable to make a strong attack on either of the first two.*

Source: "Carter at the Crossroads." TIME. *Time, Inc., July 23. 1979. Web. Accessed September 7, 2014.*

The rivalry went beyond hockey. In global politics, the United States and Soviet Union dominated. They fought together against Germany during World War II. But they became bitter foes afterward. The Soviets were the leaders of the communist world. The United States was the leader of the capitalist, or democratic, world. When it came to hockey, however, there was no question which country had the better team.

President Carter had spoken about a lack of confidence in the US economy. Brooks knew people had little hope for his US hockey team, either. But he had a belief. Brooks knew his team couldn't

US Olympic hockey coach Herb Brooks directs his players in a practice before the 1980 Winter Games in Lake Placid, New York.

win on talent alone. So he would have to build a *team*. His team would have to play together. It would have to play with heart. And it would have to work harder than any other team. If he were successful, his team might be able to win a medal. He only had to get his players to believe in themselves and not buy into that crisis of confidence.

Neal Broten, *top*, was one of 80 players invited to the Team USA tryout in July 1979 in Colorado Springs, Colorado.

CHAPTER

Uneven Rivals

The journey to the 1980 Olympics began in July 1979. Approximately 80 US hockey players arrived in Colorado Springs, Colorado. They were among many more amateur athletes in town for the annual National Sports Festival. For the hockey players, though, the festival included a tryout.

The players were divided into four teams. One team had players from the northeastern United States. Another team had players from Michigan and Wisconsin. A third team had players from Minnesota only. Players from other parts of the country were put on a fourth team. The four teams competed against each other for 10 days. US coach Herb Brooks and his assistants studied the games. They were looking for 26 players to continue.

HERB BROOKS

Herb Brooks had been a member of the 1960 US Olympic hockey team. He was ready to play in the Winter Games in Squaw Valley, California. Then he was cut from the team in the final week. The United States went on to win the gold medal. Brooks later played in the 1964 and 1968 Olympics. But he never won a gold medal as a player. Brooks went on to a successful coaching career. He led his alma mater, the University of Minnesota, from 1972 to 1979. After the 1980 Olympics, he coached four different NHL teams. Brooks also coached France (1998) and again the United States (2002) in the Olympics.

Brooks knew his University of Minnesota players best. He had coached them to national championships in 1976 and 1979. So it was of little surprise that Brooks picked nine Minnesota players to move on. Among them was William "Buzz" Schneider. He was the only returning player from the 1976 US Olympic team. Standout defensemen Mike Ramsey and Bill Baker had played for Brooks. Forwards Neal Broten and Rob McClanahan did too. In all, Minnesota players made up more than one-third of the total squad.

The University of Wisconsin had won the 1977 title. Boston University followed in 1978. The bulk of the squad came from those schools and Minnesota. Center Mark Johnson and defenseman Bob Suter were among the Wisconsin Badgers who moved on. Defenseman Jack O'Callahan, forwards Mike Eruzione and Dave Silk, and goalie Jim Craig came from Boston University.

Most of the US players were still in college. A few had recently graduated or played with amateur club teams. The average age of the players was approximately 21. Many of them were unlikely ever to move on to the NHL.

No Soviets played in the NHL, either. Their country didn't allow them to. The players were probably good enough, though. Many of the Soviet players were older than the US Olympic players. Some had been playing professionally for as many as 10 years. But they were still considered amateurs. That's because they were officially paid for being soldiers rather than hockey players. The military jobs were mostly for show, though. Boris Mikhailov was the Soviet team captain and a right winger. He said he went from a private to a lieutenant colonel without doing "any army stuff."

Instead, the Soviets spent most of their time playing hockey. They were in training camp nine months of the year. They practiced three times a day. The players rarely saw their families. When not playing with the national team, they played with Soviet club teams. Many of them played for a team called CSKA Moscow. CSKA in English stood for Central Sports Club of the Army. In the United States, it was simply known as the Red Army team.

IN THE News

Herb Brooks began putting together the US Olympic team in 1979. The difficulty of his job was not lost on him or the country. A *New York Times* story described his chances.

> Herb Brooks, a college coach from Minnesota, has a monumental task that only begins today when he chooses the players for the United States team. He will coach a group of young men—probably the youngest of any team in the entire Olympics—that will be geared to face the same Soviet squad that routed the NHL's best players in the Challenge Cup series at Madison Square Garden.

Source: Gerald Eskenazi. "An Icy Challenge Starts." New York Times, August 2, 1979. Print. D16.

The Soviet hockey system was effective. The Soviet Union first fielded a national team in 1954. It won a medal in every major tournament it entered going into the 1980 Olympics. The Soviets had won the past four Olympic titles. In addition, they had won 12 of the past 15 World Championships.

Goalie Vladislav Tretiak was the team's star. He had been the starting goalie for eight years. Hockey experts easily considered him the best goalie in the world. Soviet coach Viktor Tikhonov was

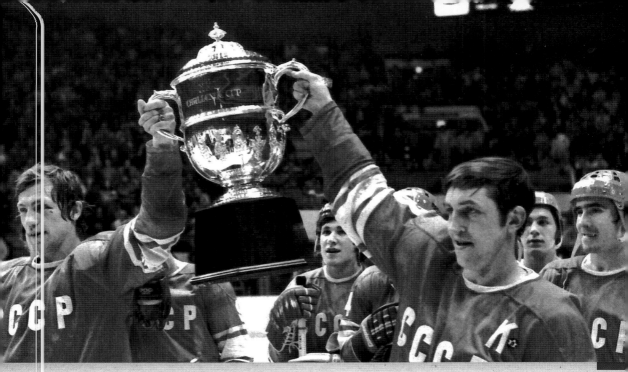

Soviet players Valeri Vasilyev, *left*, and Boris Mikhailov hold the Challenge Cup after their team beat an NHL All-Star Team in 1979 in New York City.

very strict. Many of his players disliked him. Yet they also felt the discipline was a major reason for the team's success.

The Soviets had shown their dominance in February 1979. They faced a team of NHL All-Stars in the Challenge Cup. The Soviets won two of the three games in the series. The final game was a 6–0 blowout. For the US Olympic team—a far cry from NHL All-Stars—beating the Soviets would be a huge task. But even beating Czechoslovakia or Sweden would be a big challenge. Few believed Team USA even had a chance to win a medal, let alone the gold medal.

US coach Herb Brooks, *right*, talks with goalie Jim Craig in a practice before the 1980 Olympics.

The Making of a Team

Herb Brooks had picked out 26 players. Next he had to mold them into a team. That wasn't going to be easy. The college rivalries were fierce. Many of the players disliked each other. Now they would have to play together.

To unite the players, Brooks believed they needed a common enemy. He decided to make himself that enemy. One way he did that was by using what his players called "Brooksisms." They were little sayings that insulted the players. His plans went much deeper than that, though.

The team practiced together for a month in the United States. Then it left for a three-week trip to Europe. The Americans played against other national or club teams.

Team USA won six of its first eight games. But one night the team played poorly and tied Norway 3–3. Brooks was angry.

The players and fans started leaving the arena. Brooks stopped his players. He directed them to one of the goal lines. Then he had them skate to the nearest blue line and back. Then they skated to the red line and back. Next they skated to the far blue line and back. Finally they skated to the other goal line and back. After that, they did it all over again. This continued for approximately an hour.

The fans all had left. The janitor turned off the lights. The players were skating in the dark. Brooks's message was clear. To beat the Soviets, his players would have to work harder than ever before. The next night they played Norway again. This time they won 9–0.

The US team played more games when it returned home. Brooks had worked out a deal to play against teams from the Central Hockey League (CHL). He didn't want the minor league opponents to take it easy, though. So the results would count in the CHL standings. That way the CHL teams would be motivated to win.

Brooks had 26 players on the team. He would have to cut the squad to 20 players for the Olympics. Still, he continued bringing in new players for tryouts. Then Brooks told team captain Mike Eruzione he was thinking of cutting him. Word of that discussion spread. A group of players went to Brooks. They said they had developed a trust playing together. Bringing in new players could hurt the team chemistry they had developed. Brooks got the reaction he was hoping for. The players had stood up for each other as a team. He sent the new players home and made his final cuts.

THREATS OF BOYCOTT

US-Soviet relations were already strained. Then, on Christmas Eve in 1979, the Soviet Union invaded Afghanistan. The United States was to host the Winter Games in less than two months. The Soviet Union was scheduled to host the Summer Games in July 1980. In January, President Carter threatened to boycott. He said Team USA would not participate in the Summer Games if the Soviet army remained in Afghanistan. The tensions between the two countries grew. And the Winter Games were right around the corner.

The Olympic team played 61 games in the six months leading to the Olympics. It won 42, lost 16, and tied three. But the team still had one exhibition game left to play. Brooks had scheduled a final game for three days before the Olympics. It was set for Madison Square Garden in New York City. And the Americans would face their biggest challenge yet: the Soviets.

It was a disaster. The Soviets scored early and often, and they won 10–3.

US goalie Jim Craig looks on as Rob McClanahan scrambles on the ice in the team's pre-Olympic exhibition against the Soviet Union in New York City.

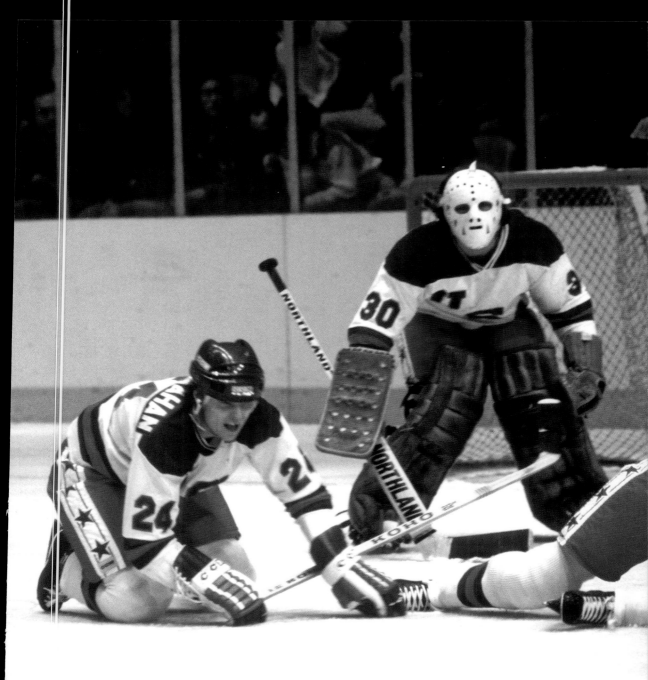

CHAPTER 4

US players Bill Baker and Mark Wells, *with puck*, skate past Sweden's Tomas Johnson, who fell, in their opening game at the 1980 Olympic Winter Games.

The Games
Begin

The Olympic Opening Ceremony was held on February 13 in the small town of Lake Placid, New York. But ice hockey began a day early so there would be enough time to play all of the games. Team USA started against Sweden. It took only 11 minutes and 4 seconds for the United States to fall behind. The score remained 1–0 until 28 seconds remained in the second period. That's when Dave Silk tied the game for Team USA.

But Sweden went back ahead 4:45 into the third period. Thomas Eriksson scored for a 2–1 lead. The United States desperately searched for a tying goal. Finally, with 41 seconds

The US dream of a gold medal at the Olympics nearly ended before it started. Sweden was considered a medal favorite. But the US players seemed to come out flat. The *New York Times* reported on the game.

> *There were long stretches when the United States forgot the intriguing style that Brooks had installed when he created this team last September. The Americans rarely moved with purpose when they did not have the puck, a key element in Brooks's new synthesis of the old and new. Instead they remembered only to play the body, slamming Swedes into the boards and corners.*

Source: Gerald Eskenazi. "Americans Tie Swedes, 2–2, On Goal in Last 27 Seconds." New York Times, February 12, 1980. Print. A1.

remaining, US coach Herb Brooks pulled goalie Jim Craig. An extra attacker took the ice as the US net sat empty.

It was a huge risk. But 14 seconds later it paid off. Mark Pavelich got the puck along the left boards. He sent a pass into the slot. Defenseman Bill Baker skated in from the blue line and one-timed a slap shot. The puck got past Sweden goalie Pelle Lindbergh to tie the game. That's how it ended.

The US players celebrate after Bill Baker scored the game-tying goal against Sweden in the 1980 Olympic opener.

Rob McClanahan scores Team USA's first goal in a 4–2 win over West Germany.

Tying the game was crucial for Team USA. Twelve teams were split into two groups. Team USA was in the Blue Division. It still had to play Czechoslovakia, Romania, West Germany, and Norway. Only the top two teams would advance to the second round.

The Soviets were in the Red Division. They began with a 16–0 win over Japan. Then they beat the Netherlands 17–4. They won all five of their division games by a combined 51–11. The favorites indeed looked unstoppable.

CCCP

The name Soviet Union was short for the Union of Soviet Socialist Republics (USSR). Russia was the largest of the 15 Soviet socialist republics and dominated the others. The Russian language uses the Cyrillic alphabet. It is an alphabet that is based from Greek. The Cyrillic alphabet makes USSR into CCCP. The Soviet Union team usually wore red or white uniforms with CCCP in block letters on the front.

The Czechs were next for the United States. And once again, the Americans fell behind. This time it took only 2:23. But Mike Eruzione tied it at 4:39 of the first period. The United States took its first lead of the Olympics a little more than a minute later. Pavelich scored the go-ahead goal. However, the Czechs tied the game 2–2 before the end of the period.

The United States was outshot 6–5 in the second period. But Buzz Schneider and Mark Johnson each scored. That put the Americans ahead 4–2. Team USA broke out in the third period. Goals by Phil Verchota, Schneider, and Rob McClanahan completed a surprising 7–3 US victory.

The win put the United States in strong position to make the medal round. Team USA again trailed in its game against Norway. But it came back to win 5–1. Then the Americans beat Romania 7–2. The final first-round game was against West Germany. Team USA went down 2–0. Again, though, the Americans came back. This time they won 4–2.

Teams received two points for a win and one for a tie. Team USA finished the first group stage with nine points. The United States and Sweden were tied atop the Blue Division. So the Americans and Swedes moved on to the medal round. The Soviet Union and Finland advanced from the Red Division.

The medal round was a second group stage. Each team played the two teams from the other division. Team USA's 2–2 tie with Sweden would carry over. Its results against the Soviet Union and Finland would be added.

The medal round began on February 22. Team USA opened against the Soviet Union. The game the Americans had spent the last six months preparing for had arrived.

US coach Herb Brooks knew his team had a major challenge awaiting against the Soviet Union.

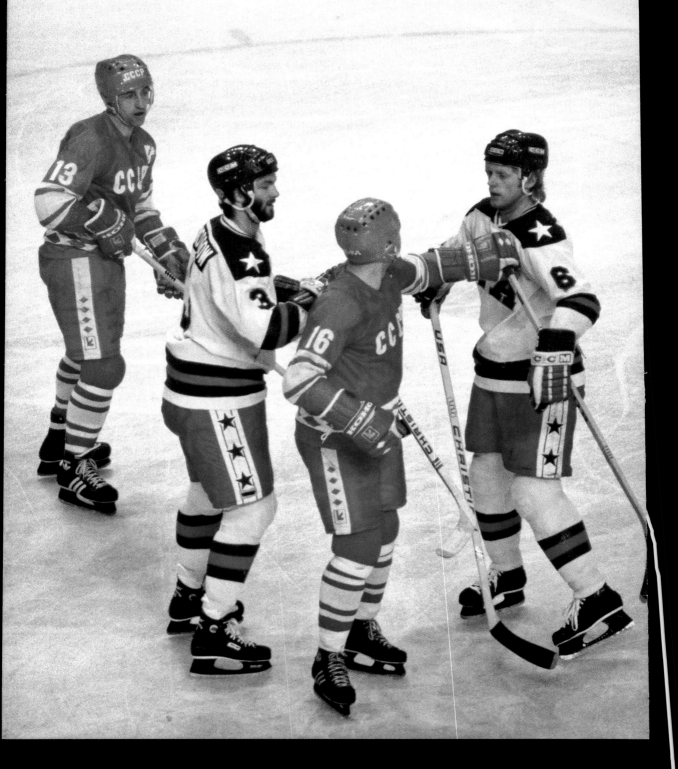

Tensions were high when the US and Soviet teams faced off in the 1980 Winter Games.

CHAPTER 5

Do You Believe in Miracles?

The United States–Soviet Union game was broadcast live in Canada. So some Americans living on the border were able to watch live. But most US viewers had to wait for the ABC broadcast. The game was scheduled for 5 p.m. on a Friday. That would be a hard time for people to tune in. So the network decided to show the game later that night on tape delay. The political history between the two countries was well known. Many Americans tuned into their first hockey game that night.

The hockey games were held in the Olympic Fieldhouse. It had been only half full for Team USA's first game against Sweden. This time it was packed. Many of the 7,700 fans wore red, white, and blue. They waved American flags.

US and Soviet players battle during their Olympic meeting in 1980.

The Soviets were still heavily favored. After all, they had dominated Team USA only a few weeks earlier in New York City. This game started much better for the Americans. But midway through the first period, that changed. Buzz Schneider lost the puck skating out from behind his own goal. Alexei Kasatonov took a slap shot from the right point. Vladimir Krutov deflected it past Jim Craig. Soviet Union 1, USA 0.

But the United States wasn't going to wilt this time. Less than five minutes later, Schneider made up for his mistake. He flew down the left wing. Just as he crossed into the Soviet zone, he took a slap shot. It beat goalie Vladislav Tretiak. Soviet Union 1, USA 1.

The Soviets kept coming, too. With 2:26 remaining in the period, they had a rush into the US zone. The puck bounced to Sergei Makarov in the slot. He scored to put the Soviets back ahead 2–1.

The Soviets had so far outplayed the Americans and outshot them 18–8. The US players fought to the end of the period, though. With time running out, Dave Christian took the puck in his own end. He skated toward center ice. As he reached the red line, he took a slap shot. Tretiak blocked it. Most of the players on both sides figured time would run out. But Mark Johnson kept playing. He skated between two Soviet defensemen, who had stopped. When he reached the puck, he slipped it around Tretiak and into the net. Soviet Union 2, USA 2. The clock showed no time left. But the goal was actually scored with one second to go.

The Soviets had mostly controlled the play. But the US players were feeling good. When they returned to the ice for the second period, they were greeted by a surprise. Soviet coach

Team USA's Rob McClanahan tries to score on Soviet goalie Vladimir Myshkin during the 1980 Olympic game.

Viktor Tikhonov had switched goalies. He thought Tretiak was playing poorly. So Vladimir Myshkin replaced Tretiak as goalie.

The Soviets picked up where they left off. Aleksandr Maltsev skated in alone on Craig and scored easily early in the period.

MIKE ERUZIONE

Mike Eruzione was Team USA's captain at the 1980 Winter Games. Few expected him to be the hero, though. The Winthrop, Massachusetts, native was 25 years old at the 1980 Olympics. He had been a star player and a leader for Boston University. However, NHL teams didn't have much interest in him. Eruzione didn't try to play professionally after the Olympics, either. He retired from hockey. Eruzione said he could never again reach those heights. He would go on to become a broadcaster on hockey games, including five Olympics. He also later returned to Boston University as an assistant hockey coach.

They went on to outshoot Team USA 12–2. But Craig made several big saves to keep the score 3–2 after two periods.

Craig continued to dominate into the third period. Then the Soviet Union's Vladimir Krutov was called for high-sticking. Team USA went on a power play. With only seconds left in the power play, Dave Silk skated across the blue line. Valeri Vasilev hip checked Silk. But the American still shot the puck toward the goal. It bounced off Soviet defenseman Sergei Starikov's stick. Then it hit his skate and deflected onto Johnson's stick. Johnson was skating ahead of the play. He quickly shot and scored. With 11:21 to go, the game was tied 3–3.

The momentum had shifted to the United States. Less than 90 seconds later, Team USA was in the Soviet zone. The puck bounced along the left boards. Mark Pavelich deflected it toward the slot.

IN THE News

After Team USA's win, President Jimmy Carter called the players in the locker room to congratulate them. As the *Washington Post* reported, some had a hard time believing what they had done.

And when it was over, it was left to Eruzione, the tough kid from Massachusetts many professional scouts say is too slow and too small to play in their league, to explain what it all meant.

"I don't think you can put it into words," he said. "It was 20 guys pulling for each other, never quitting, 60 minutes of good hockey. I don't think we kicked their butts. We just won. It's a human emotion that's indescribable."

Was it ecstasy? He was asked.

"That's not strong enough," he said. "We beat the Russians. We beat the Russians."

Source: Leonard Shapiro. "U.S. Shocks Soviets in Ice Hockey, 4–3; Eruzione Goal Hands Soviet Union 4–3 Setback." Washington Post, February 23, 1980. Print. D1.

Mike Eruzione, who had just come onto the ice, went after it. With no Soviet player around him, he took a wrist shot. It beat Myshkin. USA 4, Soviet Union 3.

The building shook. The Americans were ahead for the first time in the game.

The US players celebrate after beating the Soviet Union in the game that became known as the "Miracle on Ice."

Ten minutes remained. But that was a lot of time against the Soviets. Coach Herb Brooks repeatedly told his players, "Play your game." The Americans looked at the clock constantly. Craig again made several big saves. He had nine saves in the third period alone. As the clock ticked toward the end, Team USA still had the lead.

"You've got 10 seconds," ABC sportscaster Al Michaels screamed, trying to be heard over the deafening crowd noise. "The countdown going on right now. [Ken] Morrow, up to Silk. Five seconds left in the game. . . . Do you believe in miracles? YES!"

The United States had beaten the Soviet Union 4–3. It had accomplished one of the biggest upsets in the history of sports.

Team USA celebrates after beating Finland to win the 1980 Olympic gold medal.

CHAPTER

The Legacy

Many Americans thought the United States already had won the gold medal. But Team USA still had one game to play. And the game against Finland was a big one. Due to the unique format of the medal round, Team USA could still finish fourth with a loss.

Team USA had trailed in five of its six games so far. It again trailed against Finland. Twice. Finland took a 2–1 lead into the third period. But Phil Verchota tied the game 2:25 into the final period. Rob McClanahan put the Americans ahead less than four minutes later. Mark Johnson came through next. He scored a team-leading fifth goal with less than 3.5 minutes to go. With that, the United States beat Finland 4–2. The win secured the United States' first gold medal in ice hockey since 1960.

AT THE MOVIES

The US victory of the Soviet Union was widely celebrated at the time. It has become mythical in popular culture. Several movies have been made about it. The first was a made-for-TV film in 1981 called *Miracle on Ice*. The famous actor Karl Malden played coach Herb Brooks. Steve Guttenberg played goalie Jim Craig. In 2001, a documentary called *Do You Believe in Miracles?* aired on HBO. It included interviews with many of the players and video from the games. The most famous movie, *Miracle*, was made in 2004 with Kurt Russell as Brooks.

The reaction was almost immediate. Al Michaels's broadcast call of the final seconds of the win over the Soviet Union became iconic. People began calling the US win "The Miracle on Ice."

Thirteen of the 20 US players went on to play in the NHL. Several of them had notable careers. Ken Morrow joined the New York Islanders after the Olympics. He won the Stanley Cup later that year. Mark Johnson scored 203 goals with five NHL teams over 11 seasons.

For years, the Soviet government didn't allow its players to join the NHL. Sergei Pryakhin, who did not play in the 1980 Olympics, was the first. He played with the Calgary Flames in the 1988–89 NHL season. Five 1980 Olympians joined him one year later. They were Helmuts Balderis, Viacheslav Fetisov, Alexei Kasatonov, Vladimir Krutov, and Sergei Makarov.

The 1984 summer Olympics were held in Los Angeles, but the Soviet team did not participate. Four years earlier, the United States boycotted the 1980 Summer Games in Moscow.

The political rivalry between the United States and Soviet Union remained. After the Winter Games, focus turned to the Summer Games coming up in July in Moscow, the Soviet capital. On January 20, President Carter had demanded that the Soviet troops leave Afghanistan in one month. If not, he said Team USA would boycott the Moscow Games. The Soviets didn't budge. In fact, their troops remained in Afghanistan until 1989. Because they ignored President Carter's warning, the US Olympic team did not participate in the 1980 Summer Games. Sixty-four other nations joined the United States in the boycott. Four years later, the Soviet Union led a boycott of the 1984 Summer Games in Los Angeles. The Soviets said they feared for their athletes' safety. However, most saw the move as payback for the US-led boycott in 1980.

IN THE News

In 2005, US goalie Jim Craig wrote that the 1980 Winter Games were unique in history.

I don't believe those Winter Games in Lake Placid will ever be duplicated. I don't say that because we beat maybe the greatest Soviet hockey team ever assembled, or even because [US speedskater] Eric Heiden won five gold medals, a performance that I honestly think dwarfs what we did. I say it because there weren't doping scandals or judging scandals or an Olympic Village that was overrun with millionaires and professionals in Lake Placid.

Source: Jim Craig. Foreword. The Boys of Winter, The Untold Story of a Coach, a Dream, and the 1980 US Olympic Hockey Team. *By Wayne Coffey. New York: Crown Publishers, 2005. Print. xii.*

Much has changed both in politics and sports since 1980. The Soviet Union broke apart in 1991. It eventually became 15 separate countries. The largest is Russia.

The 1988 Summer Games were the last to be limited to amateurs. Professional basketball players made a memorable Olympic debut in 1992. The US "Dream Team" featured the best players in the world. Six years later, the NHL allowed its players to play in the 1998 Winter Games. The NHL even stopped its season so its players could compete in Nagano, Japan.

Members of the 1980 US Olympic hockey team light the cauldron at the opening ceremony for the 2002 Olympic Winter Games in Salt Lake City.

The changes mean the circumstances that led to the surprise of the 1980 US victory over the Soviet Union likely will never happen again. But there was a time, on a small rink, in a tiny town, in the mountains of New York, when a bunch of college kids beat the best ice hockey team in the world.

TIMELINE

July 27, 1979

The US National Sports Festival begins in Colorado Springs, Colorado. The ice hockey tournament serves as a tryout for the Olympic team.

August 2, 1979

US Olympic coach Herb Brooks selects a preliminary 26-man training camp roster.

November 4, 1979

Iranian radical students storm the US embassy in Tehran, taking 52 American diplomats hostage.

December 24, 1979

The Soviet Union begins its military invasion of Afghanistan.

January 20, 1980

US President Jimmy Carter announces US Olympic team will not participate in 1980 Summer Olympics in Moscow unless Soviet military forces withdraw from Afghanistan within one month.

February 9, 1980

The US Olympic hockey team loses its final Olympic preparation game to the Soviet Union 10–3 at Madison Square Garden in New York City.

February 12, 1980

The United States scores in the final minute to tie Sweden 2–2 in its first game of the Olympics.

February 13, 1980

The Olympic Winter Games officially open in Lake Placid, New York.

February 22, 1980

The United States upsets the Soviet Union 4–3 in the medal round of the Olympic ice hockey tournament.

February 24, 1980

The United States twice rallies from a one-goal deficit to beat Finland 4–2 and win the Olympic ice hockey gold medal, its first since 1960.

July 19, 1980

The summer Olympics begin in Moscow without the United States and 64 other invited nations. Four years later, the Soviet Union leads a boycott of the 1984 Olympics in Los Angeles.

allies
Countries that formally join together against a common cause.

alma mater
The school that somebody attended.

amateur
An athlete who is not allowed to be paid for competing in sports.

boycott
To refuse to participate in something as a form of protest.

check
To slow or stop a player or puck from going in a specific direction. Body checks and stick checks are examples.

faceoff
The way a hockey game is started or restarted. The referee drops the puck between two players who line up face-to-face and the players attempt to gain control of it.

high-sticking
A penalty when a player touches an opponent with his stick above the shoulder level.

hostage
Somebody held against their will.

power play
A period of time in which one team plays with more players because of a penalty called on the other team.

rivalry
A relationship between two parties that dislike each other intensely, usually due to a long history between them.

rush
When a team gains possession of the puck and moves play into the other team's end of the ice.

slap shot
When a player winds up his stick, swinging it back so that the blade comes almost even or higher than his shoulder. He brings the stick down to strike, or slap, the puck with a great deal of force.

slot
The narrow strip of ice in front of the goal between the two faceoff circles.

FOR MORE INFORMATION

SELECTED BIBLIOGRAPHY

Coffey, Wayne. *The Boys of Winter: The Untold Story of a Coach, a Dream, and the 1980 U.S. Olympic Hockey Team*. New York: Crown Publishing, 2005. Print.

Eskenazi, Gerald. "Americans Tie Swedes, 2–2, On Goal in Last 27 Seconds." *New York Times*, February 12, 1980. Print. A1.

Shapiro, Leonard. "U.S. Shocks Soviets in Ice Hockey, 4–3; Eruzione Goal Hands Soviet Union 4–3 Setback." *Washington Post*, February 23, 1980. Print. D1.

FURTHER READINGS

Gilbert, John. *Herb Brooks: The Inside Story of a Hockey Mastermind*. Minneapolis, MN: Voyageur Press, 2008. Print.

Urstadt, Brian, ed. *The Greatest Hockey Stories Ever Told*. Guilford, CT: Globe Pequot Press, 2007. Print.

Wendel, Tim. *Going for the Gold: How the U.S. Olympic Hockey Team Won at Lake Placid*. Mineola, NY: Dover Publications, 2009. Print.

WEBSITES

To learn more about the Greatest Events in Sports History, visit **booklinks.abdopublishing.com.** These links are routinely monitored and updated to provide the most current information available.

PLACES TO VISIT

Herb Brooks Arena
2634 Main Street
Lake Placid, NY 12946
(800) 462-6236
www.whiteface.com/facilities/olympic-center
Originally called the Olympic Fieldhouse, the multipurpose ice rink was the site of Team USA's 4–3 victory over the Soviet Union in the 1980 Olympic Winter Games. It was renamed for the coach of the US team, Herb Brooks, in 2005. It is one of four ice rinks within the Olympic Center complex, three indoor and one outdoor. Lake Placid also includes the Lake Placid Olympic Museum that chronicles the two Winter Games hosted by the small New York town, in 1932 and 1980.

US Hockey Hall of Fame Museum
801 Hat Trick Avenue
Eveleth, MN 55734
(800) 443-7825
www.ushockeyhall.com
The US Hockey Hall of Fame Museum is dedicated to the history of American ice hockey, with an emphasis on the sport's most memorable moments and people. It is located in Eveleth, about a three-hour drive from Minneapolis, the largest city in Minnesota. It was opened in 1973 and contains many exhibits and artifacts about American ice hockey, including an exhibit dedicated to 1980 Olympic coach Herb Brooks with many items from his personal collection. There is also the Hockey Hall of Fame in Toronto, Canada, dedicated mostly to the history of the NHL.

INDEX

ABOUT THE AUTHOR

Brian Trusdell grew up watching the Hershey Bears and has covered sports, including ice hockey, his entire journalism career, beginning in 1980 with the Pittsburgh Penguins. He covered ice hockey at the 1994 and 1998 Winter Olympics and also reported on the 1996 World Cup of Hockey for the Associated Press. He lives in New Jersey with his wife.